HABARI GANI?
(How are you?)

MAMA, BABA AND MPENDWA!
(Loved ones)

As descendants of Africa, we believe it is imperative that we create educational materials to teach our children and support our efforts to reconnect with our cultural heritage and traditions in Africa. This Counting in Kiswahili activity book is a part of that effort. It is intended to support Black children and families in learning Kiswahili words together.

We believe Black families and children should learn an African language that reflects our culture and traditions before learning foreign languages that reflect other ethnic groups' culture and traditions. Counting in Kiswahili is a fun and engaging way to support our children's numeracy development while introducing them to one of the most frequently spoken languages on the Continent.

In this book, our children will learn to count in Kiswahili and English as they learn numbers and words. They will also develop their handwriting and fine motor skills by coloring images that reflect our cultural heritage and traditions in Africa.

We are learning Kiswahili as a family. It is our hope and desire that more Black families and children will learn to speak Kiswahili, too. We invite you to learn with us.

WE HOPE YOU ENJOY THE ACTIVITIES!

There is only one Africa! Did you know our cultural heritage and traditions started in Africa? I am happy we are descendants of Africa.

moja means one

Trace the Number 1

Write the Number 1

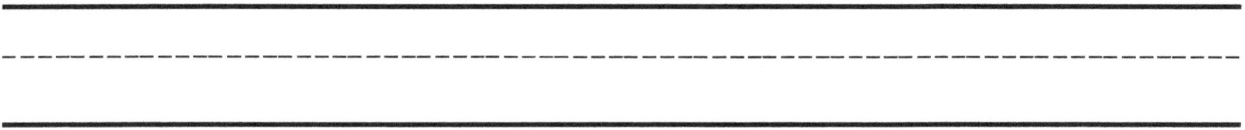

Trace the English Word for the Number 1: one

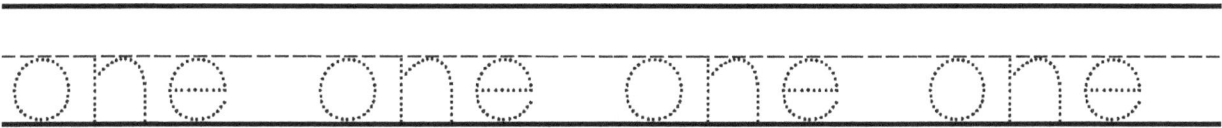

one one one one

Write the English Word for the Number 1: one

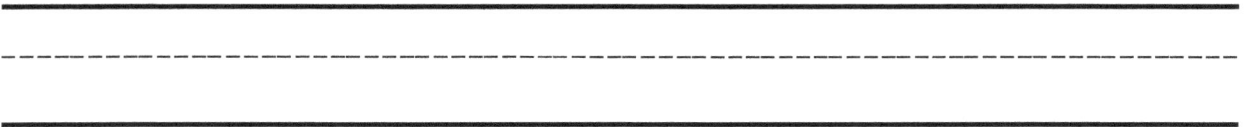

Trace the Kiswahili Word for the Number 1: moja   (Pronounced mo-jah)

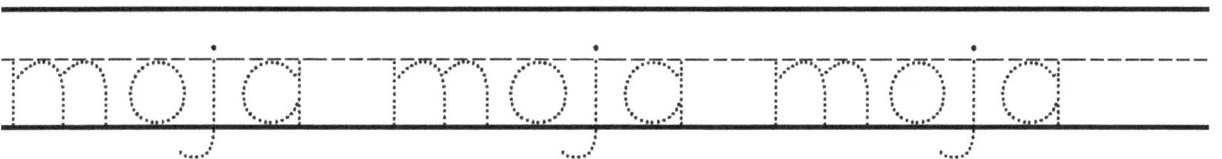

moja moja moja

Write the Kiswahili Word for the Number 1: moja

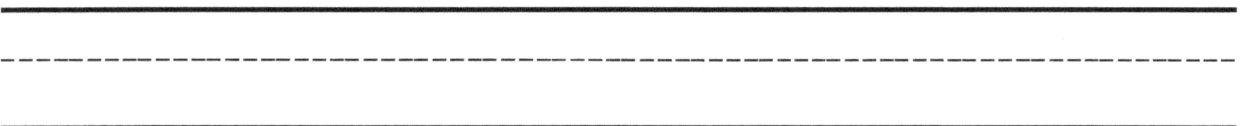

I love playing mankala with my friend Hakim. We taught everyone in our school how to play the game.

How many players do you see in the picture?

mbili means two

Trace the Number 2

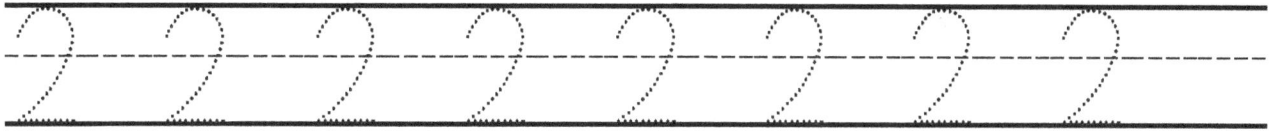

2 2 2 2 2 2 2 2 2

Write the Number 2

Trace the English Word for the Number 2: two

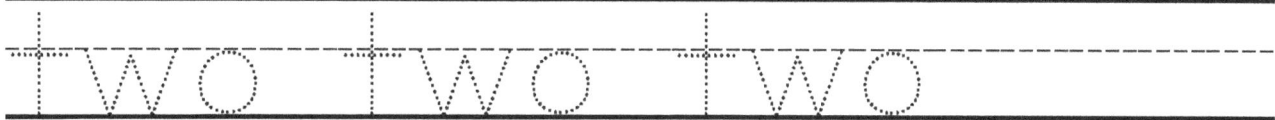

two two two

Write the English Word for the Number 2: two

Trace the Kiswahili Word for the Number 2: mbili   (Pronounced m-bee-lee)

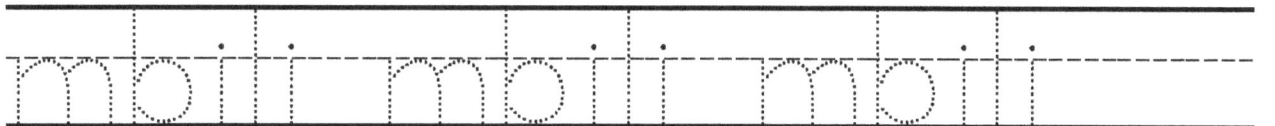

mbili mbili mbili

Write the Kiswahili Word for the Number 2: mbili

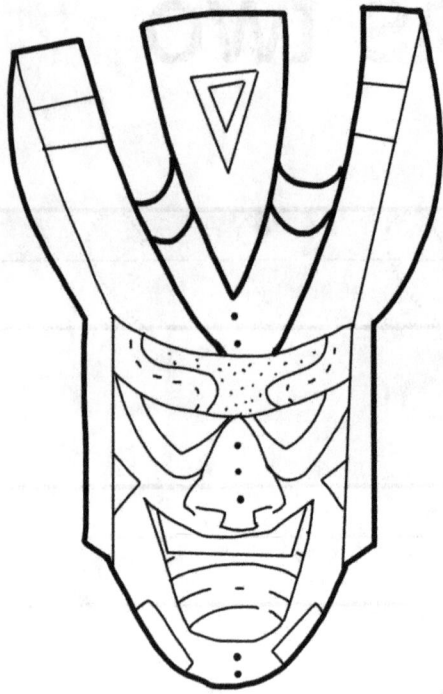

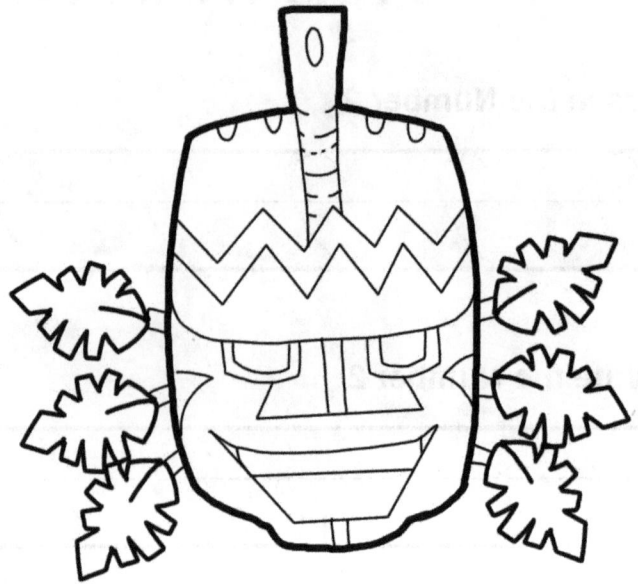

There are three African masks on the wall in my house. I like to put them on my face. Count the masks in the picture.

tatu means three

Trace the Number 3

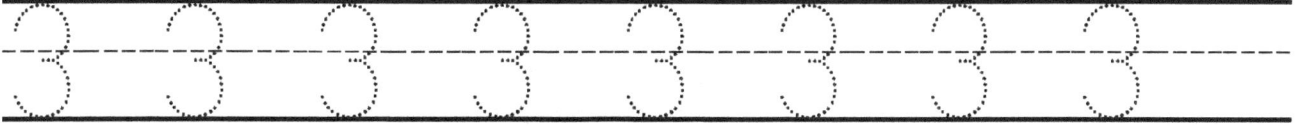

3 3 3 3 3 3 3 3

Write the Number 3

Trace the English Word for the Number 3: three

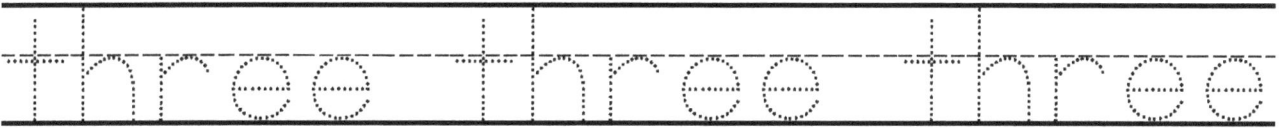

three three three

Write the English Word for the Number 3: three

Trace the Kiswahili Word for the Number 3: tatu   (Pronounced ta-too)

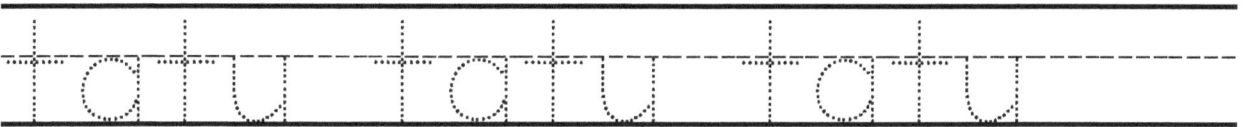

tatu tatu tatu

Write the Kiswahili Word for the Number 3: tatu

I have four African drums that I like to play. Do you like playing the drums?
Count the drums in the picture.

nne means four

Trace the Number 4

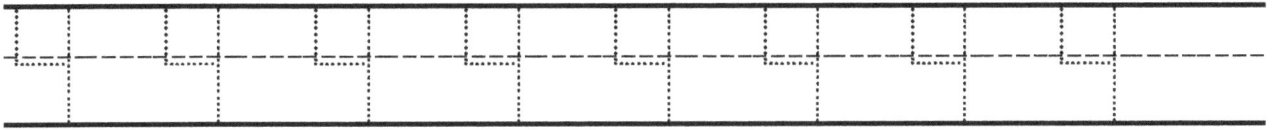

Write the Number 4

Trace the English Word for the Number 4: four

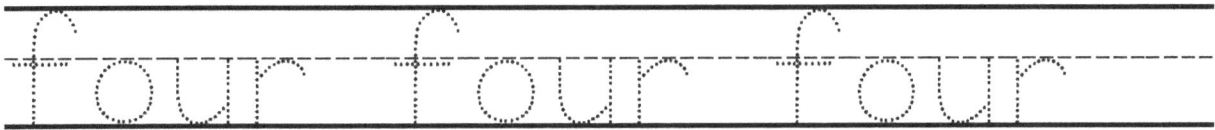

four four four

Write the English Word for the Number 4: four

Trace the Kiswahili Word for the Number 4: nne   (Pronounced n-nay)

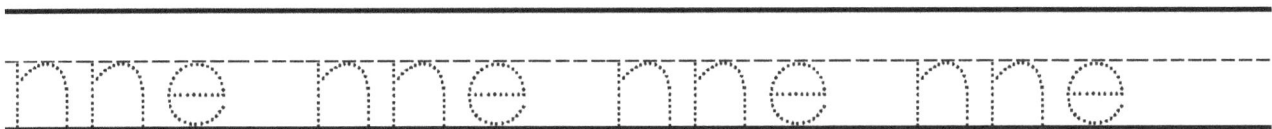

nne   nne   nne   nne

Write the Kiswahili Word for the Number 4: nne

Playing African warriors is so much fun!
Do you want to play with us?
How many shields are in the picture?
How many spears are in the picture?

tano means five

Trace the Number 5

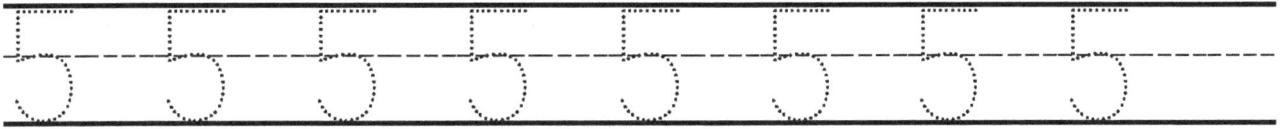

5 5 5 5 5 5 5 5 5

Write the Number 5

Trace the English Word for the Number 5: five

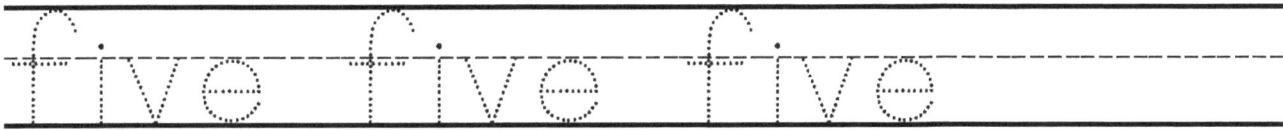

five five five

Write the English Word for the Number 5: five

Trace the Kiswahili Word for the Number 5: tano   (Pronounced tah-no)

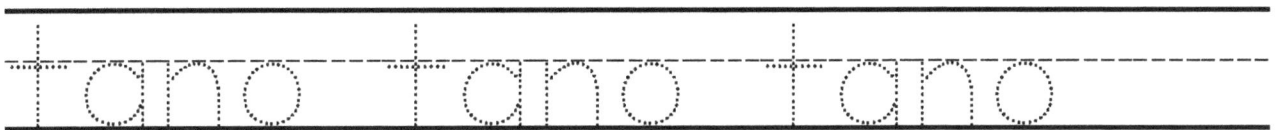

tano tano tano

Write the Kiswahili Word for the Number 5: tano

www.kujichaguliapress.com

I love eating bananas, especially ones from Tanzania.
Do you like bananas? How many bananas are in the picture?
Do you want one? Bananas are good for us!

sita means six

Trace the Number 6

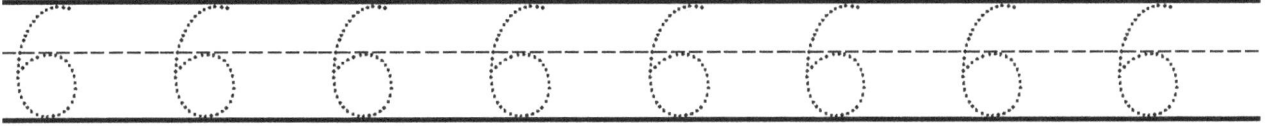

6 6 6 6 6 6 6 6

Write the Number 6

Trace the English Word for the Number 6: six

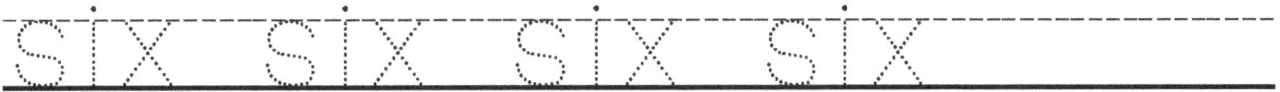

six six six six

Write the English Word for the Number 6: six

Trace the Kiswahili Word for the Number 6: sita   (Pronounced see-tah)

sita sita sita

Write the Kiswahili Word for the Number 6: sita

NGUZO SABA

1. UMOJA
2. KUJICHAGULIA
3. UJIMA
4. UJAMAA
5. NIA
6. KUUMBA
7. IMANI

Do you know the Nguzo Saba (the seven principles of Blackness)? We should practice these principles in our everyday lives.

Do you know who created the Nguzo Saba? You're right, Dr. Maulana Karenga!

saba means seven

Trace the Number 7

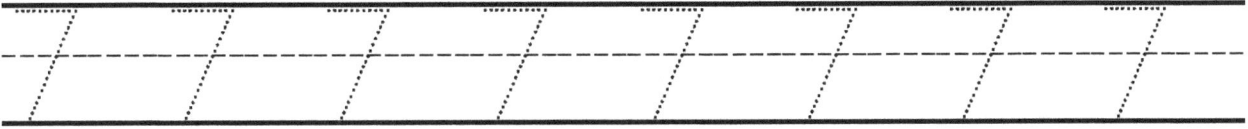

7 7 7 7 7 7 7 7

Write the Number 7

Trace the English Word for the Number 7: seven

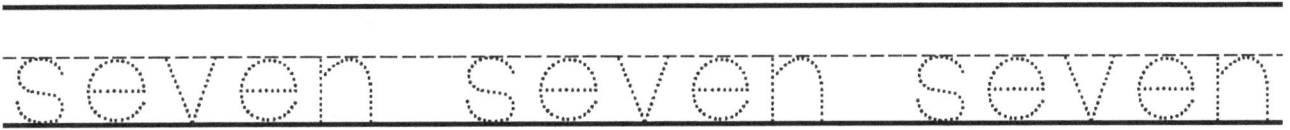

seven seven seven

Write the English Word for the Number 7: seven

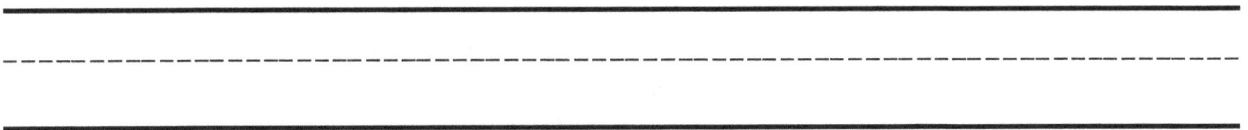

Trace the Kiswahili Word for the Number 7: seven   (Pronounced sah-bah)

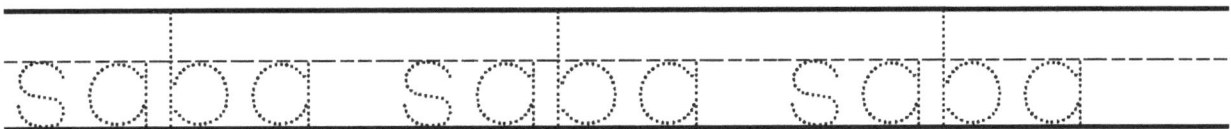

saba saba saba

Write the Kiswahili Word for the Number 7: saba

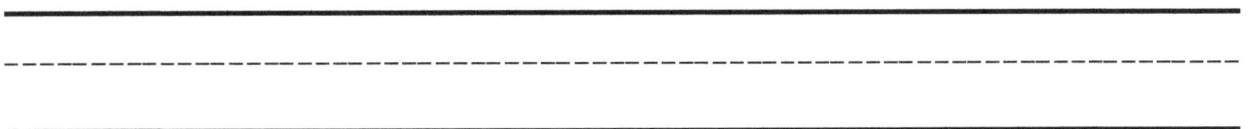

BLACK HISTORY

B I N G O

B	I	N	G	O
CIVIL RIGHTS	AFRICA	KINGS	JAZZ	EQUALITY
	AFRICA			CIVIL RIGHTS
JAZZ		FREE	CIVIL RIGHTS	AFRICA
	RIGHTS		BLACKNESS	SOUL
SOUL	EQUALITY	JAZZ		

I really like playing Black History Bingo to learn about our history. Do you want to play with me?

How many ancestors are circled on the Black History Bingo card? Can you name each ancestor?

nane means eight

Trace the Number 8

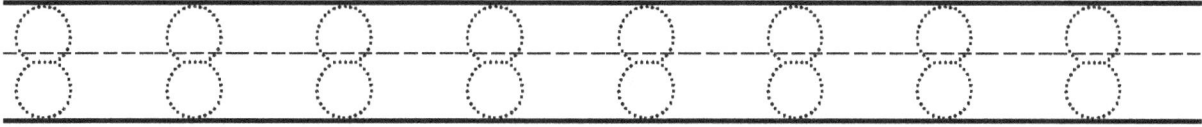

8 8 8 8 8 8 8 8

Write the Number 8

Trace the English Word for the Number 8: eight

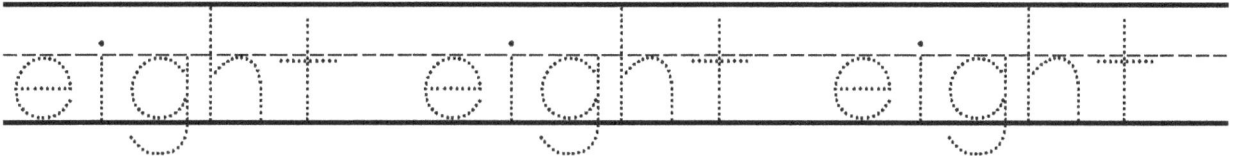

eight eight eight

Write the English Word for the Number 8: eight

Trace the Kiswahili Word for the Number 8: eight   (Pronounced nah-nay)

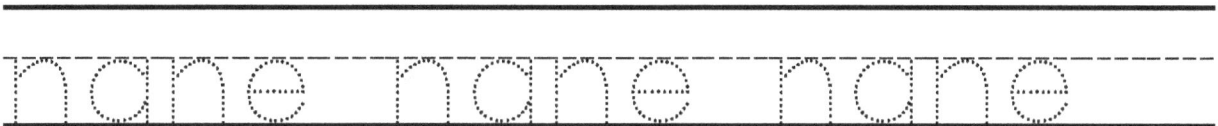

nane nane nane

Write the Kiswahili Word for the Number 8: nane

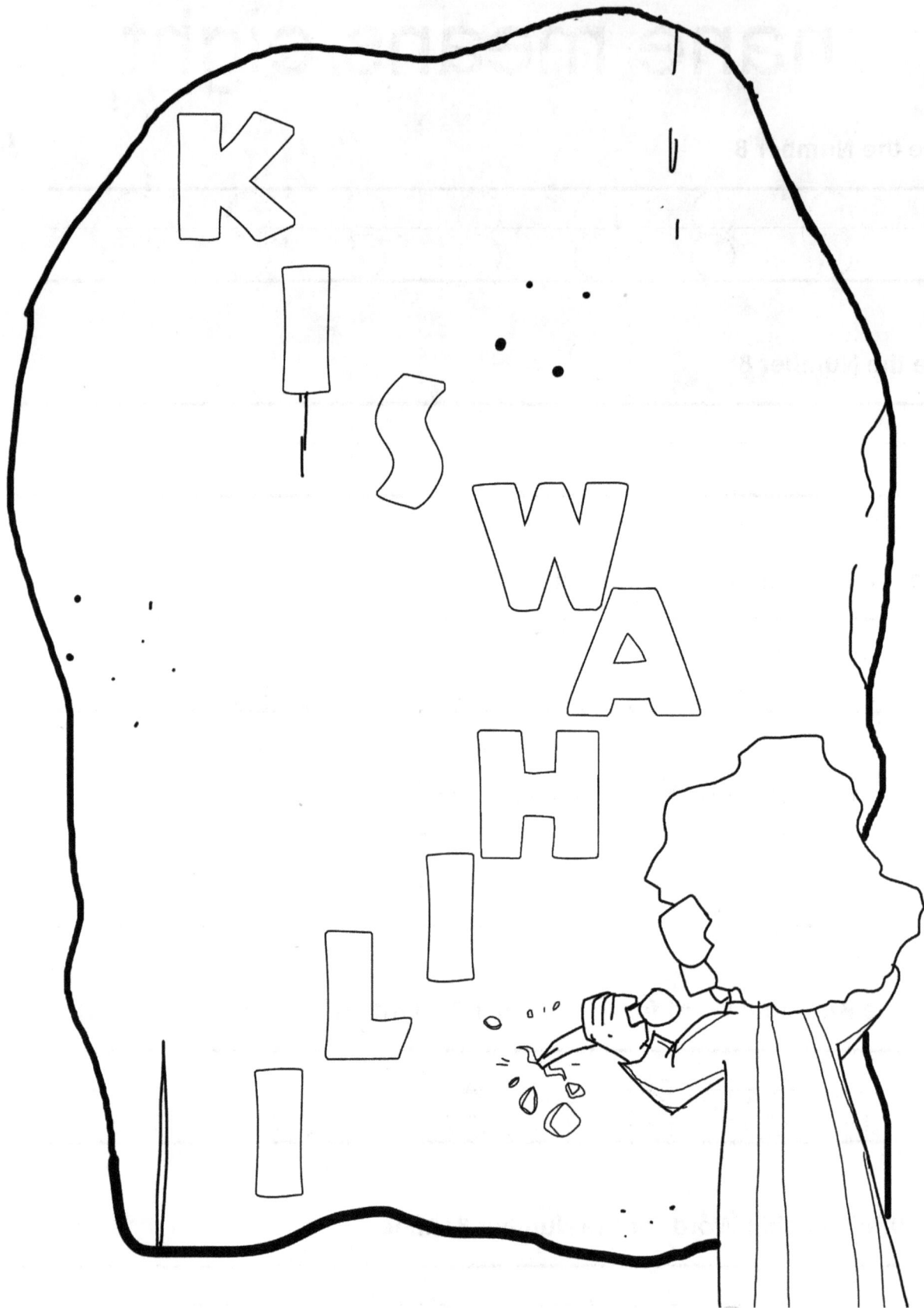

Kiswahili is an African language I am learning at school and with my family.
Do you know any Kiswhaili words? How many letters are in the word Kiswahili?

tisa means nine

Trace the Number 9

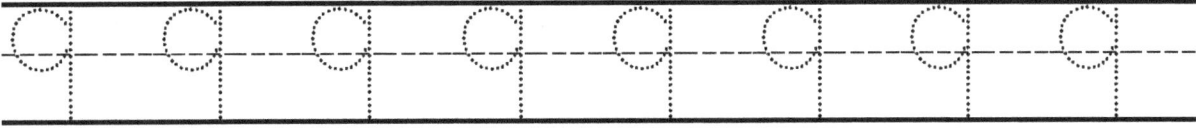

9 9 9 9 9 9 9 9 9

Write the Number 9

Trace the English Word for the Number 9: nine

nine nine nine nine

Write the English Word for the Number 9: nine

Trace the Kiswahili Word for the Number 9: nine   (Pronounced tee-sah)

tisa tisa tisa tisa

Write the Kiswahili Word for the Number 9: tisa

I love listening to our elders tell stories about Africa and our great African ancestors.

How many children are listening to the story in the picture? Do you like the stories?

kumi means ten

Trace the Number 10

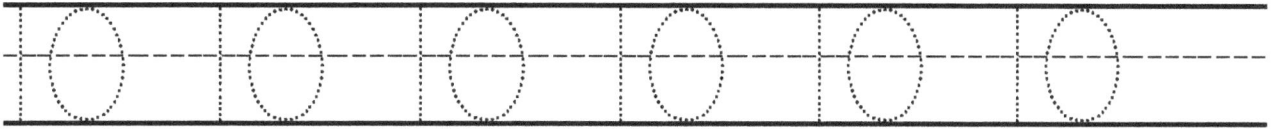

10 10 10 10 10 10 10

Write the Number 10

Trace the English Word for the Number 10: ten

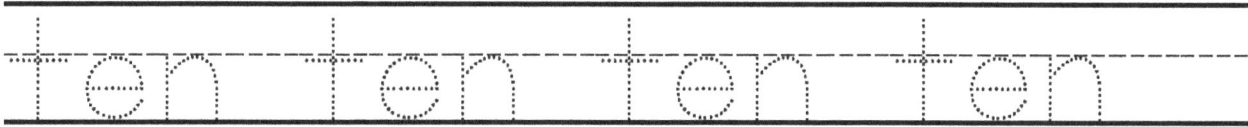

ten ten ten ten

Write the English Word for the Number 10: ten

Trace the Kiswahili Word for the Number 10: ten   (Pronounced koo-mee)

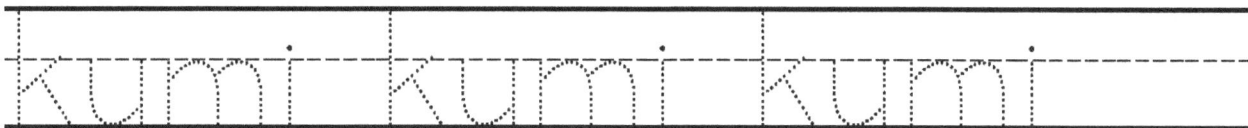

kumi kumi kumi

Write the Kiswahili Word for the Number 10: kumi

Kiswahili Review

moja

Trace the sentence below

moja means one

Write the sentence above

What number is moja? _____

Circle the number moja

1 2 3 4 5 6 7 8 9 10

Practice writing the number one (1) in Kiswahili

mbili

Trace the sentence below

mbili means two

Write the sentence above

What number is mbili? _____

Circle the number mbili

1 2 3 4 5 6 7 8 9 10

Practice writing the number two (2) in Kiswahili

tatu

Trace the sentence below

tatu means three

Write the sentence above

What number is tatu? _____

Circle the number tatu

1 2 3 4 5 6 7 8 9 10

Practice writing the number three (3) in Kiswahili

www.kujichaguliapress.com

nne

Trace the sentence below

nne means four

Write the sentence above

_____

- -

_____

What number is nne?   _____

Circle the number nne

1 2 3 4 5 6 7 8 9 10

Practice writing the number four (4) in Kiswahili

_____

- -

_____

- -

_____

tano

Trace the sentence below

tano means five

Write the sentence above

What number is tano? _____

Circle the number tano

1 2 3 4 5 6 7 8 9 10

Practice writing the number five (5) in Kiswahili

sita

Trace the sentence below

sita means six

Write the sentence above

What number is sita? _____

Circle the number sita

1 2 3 4 5 6 7 8 9 10

Practice writing the number six (6) in Kiswahili

saba

Trace the sentence below

saba means seven

Write the sentence above

_____

- -

_____

What number is saba?   _____

Circle the number saba

1 2 3 4 5 6 7 8 9 10

Practice writing the number seven (7) in Kiswahili

_____

- -

_____

_____

- -

_____

nane

Trace the sentence below

nane means eight

Write the sentence above

What number is nane? _____

Circle the number nane

1 2 3 4 5 6 7 8 9 10

Practice writing the number eight (8) in Kiswahili

tisa

Trace the sentence below

tisa means nine

Write the sentence above

What number is tisa? _____

Circle the number tisa

1 2 3 4 5 6 7 8 9 10

Practice writing the number nine (9) in Kiswahili

kumi

Trace the sentence below

kumi means ten

Write the sentence above

What number is kumi? _____

Circle the number kumi

1 2 3 4 5 6 7 8 9 10

Practice writing the number ten (10) in Kiswahili

CULTURALLY UPLIFTING FAMILY WORK!

Black Families should take an active role in helping our children develop practical, procedural, and conceptual understanding of mathematics, positive mathematics identities, and positive feelings about their abilities to do mathematics. In spite of the negative messages about our children's abilities, they are more than capable of doing mathematics! Let us repeat this: Our children are more than capable of doing mathematics! Do not fall into the trap of believing that our children cannot do or achieve in mathematics, or in any other area for that matter.

We have to engage them early on in culturally uplifting mathematics activities that incorporate their culture and interests as well as strengthen their ability to do mathematics before they enter school. We must continue these efforts throughout their schooling experience. We humbly present these culturally uplifting learning activities for you to engage in with your child (and by yourself):

1. Self-Assessment: Think about your mathematics experiences in school. Did you like mathematics? Why? Did you dislike mathematics? Why? Do you like or dislike mathematics now? It is important that you explore your experiences in mathematics so you don't transfer any dislikes or negative feelings about mathematics to your child. You have to work through any dislikes to make sure you help your child to like mathematics and develop positive attitudes and identities.

2. Tell your child how much you like mathematics on a regular basis. In our society and schools, Black children receive many negative messages about their ability to do mathematics. We have to counter and challenge those messages by providing positive messages that are stronger and louder.

3. Teach your child to identify, say and write numbers and number words. Remember, children need to practice identifying, saying, and writing numbers on a regular basis to learn them.

4. Incorporate numbers and counting into your daily routine with your child. Point at and count common objects around the house and outside in the community. Be sure to focus on objects your child likes. Have your child count with you, and engage him or her by asking questions about what they counted.

5. Read your child books that discuss mathematics topics and concepts (e.g., numbers and counting, etc.). Find books that feature Black culture and characters. Engage your child in the mathematics activities from the books while pointing at and counting the objects on each page. Discuss the books with your child.

6. In our culture, oral tradition is important. Teach your child songs, poems, stories, and rhymes about numbers and counting. You can add and take away objects to go along with the story. Be sure to include Black cultural symbols and characters in the activities.

7. Provide your child with puzzles involving numbers, counting, and other problem solving activities. Encourage your child to identify and count as he/she completes the puzzle.

8. Expose your child to fractions early and help them develop an interest in and comfort working with numbers. Use measuring cups, tape measure, blocks, and other items to help your children develop a firm understanding of what numbers and fractions are and why they are important. Give your child a ruler, tape measure, and other measuring tools to measure things around the house.

ABOUT THE AUTHORS

The Sekou Family is a Black family that lives in Baltimore, Maryland. They believe in the importance of Black families and children connecting, honoring and respecting our cultural heritage and traditions in Africa, America, the Caribbean, and the Diaspora. As a family, we work hard to learn about our cultural heritage and traditions. We practice the Nguzo Saba (The 7 Principles of Blackness) in our everyday lives and give back to our community.

The stories presented in our books are fictionalized accounts based on real events in our family and our journey to live a life that connects, honors, and respects our cultural heritage and traditions. Reading should be a regular occurrence in Black families, and it is important for Black children to see images that look like them in the books they read.

Becoming parents and watching our son, Sekou, grow up inspired these books and the stories in them. Sekou is co-author because he has contributed greatly to the books. Mama and Baba use his name as co-authors of the books to honor his contributions. We use Afrika as our last name to represent our quest to positively uplift our cultural heritage and traditions originating in Africa. Sekou has inspired us to live a life that more closely reflects our beliefs and political ideology. We strongly believe we have to create Black institutions to positively uplift Black families and children, and connect them to their cultural heritage and traditions.

Baba Sekou Afrika, Ed.D. (also known as Julius Davis) is an assistant professor of mathematics education at Bowie State University. His scholarship and advocacy focuses on the intellectual and social development of Black boys and young men. He has studied and traveled to Malawi, Tanzania, and Ethiopia on the continent of Africa to learn more about our cultural heritage and traditions.

Mama Sekou Afrika (also known as Yolanda Davis) is a clinical research professional who has studied and traveled to Senegal on the continent of Africa and the Caribbean Islands to learn more about our cultural heritage and traditions.

Sekou Afrika (also known as Sekou Davis) is a student at Ujamaa Shule, the oldest independent Afrikan School in the United States. He plays the Afrikan drums with his brothers and sisters at Ujamaa. To start his formal school-based academic and social development, Sekou attended Watoto Development Center in Baltimore, MD, an Afrikan-centered institution.

Asante Sana (Thank you very much) for practicing Ujamaa (cooperative economics) by purchasing this book and supporting our Black-owned family business. A portion of the proceeds from this book will be used to support and sponsor efforts to culturally uplift Black children and families.

Your Support is Greatly Appreciated!

Baba Sekou Afrika, Mama Sekou Afrika, Sekou Afrika

KISWAHILI GLOSSARY

We believe Black families and children should learn one or more African languages that reflect our culture and traditions before learning foreign languages that reflect other ethnic groups' cultures and traditions. As a family, we are learning Kiswahili, a language spoken across more countries in Africa than any other language. It is our hope and desire that more Black families and children will learn to speak Kiswahili. We invite you to learn Kiswahili with us:

Baba – Father.

Habari Gani – How are you?

Imani – Faith. It is one of the seven principles of Blackness.

Mama – Mother.

Mbili – Two.

Moja – One

Mpendwa – Loves ones.

Nane – Eight.

Nguzo Saba – The seven principles of Blackness.

Ninakupenda – I love you.

Nne – Four.

Kujichagulia – Self-determination. It is one of the seven principles of Blackness.

Kumi – Ten.

Kuumba – Creativity. It is one of the seven principles of Blackness.

Nia – Purpose. It is one of the seven principles of Blackness.

Sita – Six.

Saba – Seven.

Tano – Five.

Tatu – Three.

Tisa – Nine.

Ujamaa – Cooperative economics. It is one of the seven principles of Blackness.

Ujima – Collective work and responsibility. It is one of the seven principles of Blackness.

Umoja – Unity. It is one of the seven principles of Blackness.

KUJICHAGULIA PRESS

We define, speak and create for ourselves to celebrate our African and African American cultural heritage and uplift our people using our Kuumba (creativity).

Title: Counting in Kiswahili
Written by: Baba Sekou Afrika, Mama Sekou Afrika, and Sekou Afrika
Illustrated By: Eloy Claudio
Edited by : Nadirah Angail
Book Design By: Eloy Claudio

Summary: In this book, our children will learn Kiswahili number words, English numbers and words, and how to count. The book will also help our children develop their handwriting and coloring skills through practice.

ISBN: 978-0-9964595-1-8

For more information or to book an event,
contact Baba/Mama Sekou at books@kujichaguliapress.com.

Kujichagulia Press
P.O. Box 31766
Baltimore, MD 21207
www.kujichaguliapress.com

KujichaguliaPress   KujichaguliaPress   @Kujichaguliaprs

#CountingInKiswahili
#LearnKiswahili

www.ingramcontent.com/pod-product-compliance
Lightning Source LLC
Chambersburg PA
CBHW080940030426
42339CB00008B/471